AFFIRMATIONS TO THE GAME OF LIFE

by Derrick L. Frazier

www.justderrick.com

ISBN: 979-8-66267-109-6

First Published in 2020

Printed in the USA

AFFIRMATIONS TO THE GAME OF LIFE

f Derrick L. Frazier

📷 Derrick L. Frazier

website: www.justderrick.com

Illustrated by : Donald Benedict
(@donnieben.draws)

- DEDICATION -

I want to thank God for giving me the desire
to write and finish this book for my little
brothers and little sisters.
It was a very hard but fun process.
Nonetheless, Donald Benedict,
who did the illustrations for this book
as we continued to push each other daily.
So to you, my brother,
I would like to say thank you for enduring
with me.
Let's make history and save lives.

- I AM ATTRACTIVE -

You are attractive!
I used to get picked on
all the time growing up because I have a big
nose. But having a big nose, being tall with big feet,
and having a loud voice is how I was created,
and I was created for a reason.
Big or small body parts do not make you
more or less attractive. Love your mouth, nose,
eyes, ears, and your weight.
No skin color is better than another skin color
so love the skin you are in.
ALL skin colors are dope.
Love how you look and know that you are not ugly,
but you are ATTRACTIVE!

- I AM BLESSED -

You may not have the latest Jordans,
Nike Lebrons, or iPhone. Your family may not
have a lot of cash, be able to afford a big house,
or the hottest car. You may not wake
up to shrimp and grits, but,
if you have food, water, clothes,
and a roof over your head,
know that you are BLESSED.
Some kids grow up and their whole goal every day is just
to find water. So, if for now,
all you can say is that you have food, water,
and clothes on your back,
know that you are BLESSED.

- I WILL BE CONSISTENT -

Discover your God-given gifts.
Find a sport, find a hobby,
find something that you love to do,
and be CONSISTENT at learning whatever that passion is.
Study how you can make money from that gift.
Find a way to not only better yourself,
but help other people be better
at that thing you love to do.
Remember nothing happens overnight,
but with time, you will see results.
STAY CONSISTENT!

I AM DETERMINED

Be DETERMINED to do more than just exist.
Be determined to make a difference in the world.
Create something new, invent something new,
discover something new. Own a gas station,
own your land, own some tools
that will always make you legal money.
Be DETERMINED TO WIN IN LIFE
and don't expect anything to be handed to you.

I WILL EDUCATE MYSELF

I'm all for going to school but school is not the only place
that you can educate yourself.
You can educate yourself by going to Google and typing in
"how to own a business" or "how to make money as a kid."
If you ask Google, it will give you a lot of useful information.
Another one of my favorite resources is YouTube.
I'm a visual learner so,
when I want to learn how to do something,
I'll go to YouTube and find a video that will
teach me what I want to learn.
I've learned how to tie a tie, cook, do math, and so many
other things just by watching YouTube.
You can do the same thing.
However, there are some things that you can't learn in school
or on Google. Work to educate yourself on the value of money,
the value of life, how to love yourself,
and why you were created.
The more you know, the more you can grow
and the more valuable you will be in life.

I WILL FOCUS ON **THE** FOCUS

It is so easy to get distracted.
You can get distracted by spending too much time
scrolling up and down your newsfeed on Facebook or Instagram.
You can get distracted by getting caught up in a good TV series
on Netflix or even playing video games.
Dating and especially unhealthy relationships
can be a huge distraction.
When you have goals, you must lock in on those goals
and stay tunnel-vision focused.
When it gets hard, keep suiting up and showing up.
One day it will pay off.
STAY FOCUSED ON THE FOCUS!

- I AM A GIVER -

As corny as this may sound,
giving is a very good thing to do.
I look at giving as planting a seed.
There are many forms of giving.
You can give an encouraging word to someone.
You can give a hand to someone
who may need your help.
Money is ALWAYS a good way to give.
If you plant seeds and give a lot to people,
it will come back to you when you least expect it.
A wise person once said, "It is better to give than
to receive."

- I LOVE TO HU$TLE -

I swear I am giving y'all all the game in this book,
that's how much I LOVE YOU AND WANT YOU TO WIN!
Find yourself a legal hustle, something that you can always earn
money from, and work at it every day. For starters,
you can find yourself a mower and go knock on people's door in the
summertime and ask to cut their grass for $20. Once you make $20,
go to Walmart and get a gas can for about $5 bucks.
Go to your nearest gas station, fill it up for about two or three dollars
and go back to knocking on doors. It works,
I did the same thing growing up. You can even go to Dollar Tree
to buy a $1 sponge and start washing cars.

In the Fall, go door to door asking your neighbors to rake leaves.
A lot of people don't like raking leaves so I guarantee a lot of people
will let you rake their yard.

Young ladies, you could learn how to braid hair or sweep up a salon.
Ask your neighbor if you can babysit for a couple of hours.
If you are good at a school subject that your friend maybe is failing,
offer to help, but they'll have to pay you a couple of dollars.

Again, if these don't work for you, use that phone of yours
and google side hustles or how to make money as a teen or kid.
There is a hustle in you so find it and get that bag.

I WILL BE INDEPENDENT

Do not depend on a man or woman to take care of you.
Do your best to put yourself in a position in which
you don't need a man or woman to take care of
or do anything for you. When you are independent,
no one can tell you what to do and they definitely cannot
take anything from you.
For you young men, it may be easy
to let a woman to take care of you, but that is not a woman's job.
The same goes for you young ladies, you don't
need any boy buying you things just to get with you.
Material things come and go. I know many of you lack
mothers and fathers and you want that hole in your heart
to be filled, I understand. I have been there.
If you let someone else take care of you but you
know that's not what you want,
you will feel indebted to them from the moment you
decide to move on and be independent.
So, that's why I am telling you now while you're
young to learn to be independent from the start.
You will have so much more peace.

- I HAVE A LOT OF JOY -

Man, listen to me. Life is real, you feel me?
You will have days where you may not feel
like going to school or work.
Unfortunately, you will at some point experience death in
your family.
You will have some days where people will try you.
But at the end of the day, life goes on.
Don't sweat the small things in life.
Learn to live and have joy no matter what goes on around you.
If you have people around you with bad energy and
they are not making progress in life, then cut them off.
Find yourself some positive people to be around
or just do what I do and start riding alone until you find those
positive people.
Don't make room for negative people in your life.
One thing I do to bring myself laughter and joy
is listening to pranks calls and comedians roasting people in the
audience. I don't know what brings you joy,
but hopefully, you will find it and do it every
day.

- I WILL BE KIND-HEARTED -

Some of you may struggle with this one
because you have been hurt so much.
You've been let down over and over again
by your dad or mom.
You were counting on your dad to come to pick you up
for the summer but they didn't come through.
Some of y'all have been hurt by other people
who made you promises and did not come through.
Being kind doesn't take a lot but it will carry you
A LONG WAY in life.
Being kind-hearted does not mean letting people
walk over you or disrespect you,
but I am telling you that the small principles,
such as being kind to other people,
can open up so many doors and
opportunities for you.

- I AM LOVED -

Even if you don't hear it a lot, know that you are loved.
I wrote this book from my heart to help you.
I want you to know that your creator loves you and again,
I love you. It may be that you would like to hear
your mom or dad say it more.
Trust me, it would've been nice to hear
my momma say it more often too.
Somethings are just out of our control.
Another person can say they love you all day long but,
when that "I love you" comes from the lips of your
momma or daddy MY GOD it's like you get
goosebumps and chills all over your skin.
To hear your parents say, "I love you"
can never be compared to another person saying it to you.
YOU ARE NOT ALONE. I'm right here with you
praying for you and cheering you on.

I WILL MAKE A DIFFERENCE

Do not make the mistake that a lot of people do and live just to survive.
Do not just exist in this world. Make a difference.
There are a lot of problems in our world and you have it
in you to help make a difference just like I'm doing.
I realized that there are not enough small, easy-to-read books for teenagers
so I decided to write a book that children and teens can relate too.
Writing a book may not be how you make a difference. It may be
becoming a policymaker to bring more recreation to your community
or starting life skill programs in the school system to help kids
become successful entrepreneurs. You might want to open
a homeless shelter so people won't have to keep sleeping
under the bridge in the cold.
I don't know how or what you will do to make a difference,
but hopefully, you find a way and get to it.

LISTEN PLEASE! I don't know one person that is successful who never thought about giving up at least once. Why? Because life will not always go as we had written down or planned out. Life is known for throwing a lot of curveballs. It is in those difficult times that your WHY has to be greater than the option of giving up. If whatever you're doing doesn't go as planned, start over and try it again. But please, DO NOT GIVE UP! With hard work and determination, YOUR GOAL IS POSSIBLE!

I WILL NEVER GIVE UP

- I WILL OVERCOME -

You may be struggling with depression, smoking weed,
drinking alcohol, school, thoughts of self-harm,
your sexuality. Maybe you're struggling with your mindset.
Let me be the first to say, I feel you. You are not alone.
I wrestle with my thoughts and past every day.
I have been hurt by people too.
I have had my share of addictions too.
Staying focused at school was very hard for me also.
We all have things that we need to overcome.
But with much prayer and help from our family and friends,
WE WILL OVERCOME.

EPRESSION

SUICIDAL THOUGHTS

- I WILL PERSEVERE -

I know it gets real in your life.
I know you think no one understands or cares about your
struggles.
You probably have asked God 100 times, "why me though?"
I feel you, and I've asked the same questions.
I've been so low in life.
One day I remember crying out to God in
an apartment in Jacksonville, Florida,
and I told Him that I did not want to speak, preach,
or do anything anymore.
But every time I turned on the news and saw
another child fall into a life of crime
or two teens having a shootout and one dying,
I knew I couldn't give up. I care so much, y'all, for real.
I cannot stress it enough, life will try every human being
with a living soul.
But you must be determined to persevere until
the storm is over.

- I AM NOT A QUITTER -

One of the worse things you can do in life is quit.
You may be getting Fs or Ds on your report card.
It's cool, well, Fs are not cool, but, if you do get Fs it's not
the end of the world because you can bring that F up to a
passing grade by studying every day.
Maybe you are working on a project and it seems
like you just cannot figure it out,
KEEP TRYING over and over and over again.
If you have taken a school test, ASVAB test,
SAT, or any test and you have failed multiple times,
KEEP TRYING OVER AND OVER AGAIN until you pass.
You see, the best part of climbing the mountain is not the top of
the mountain, but the climb going up, knowing that you had to
climb over little and big rocks to get to the top.
It is the trees on the mountain that you had to walk around to get
to the top of the mountain.aIt is those moments,
when that mountain got a little harder to
climb as you were getting closer to the top,
when you didn't give up.
The top of the mountain is just the icing on the cake.
So, as you go through life, just take one careful
step each day and before long you'll safely arrive
at the top of your mountain, which is your life destination

- I LOVE READING -

Reading can be fun and can teach you a lot of new things.
Some of you might think that reading is boring,
which can be true if you are reading a book that doesn't interest you.
One thing that helped me to start reading was reading
small books on topics I like.
I like reading books that are short, positive, self-help books,
so that's what I write.
I like reading articles and short biographies on other people
who were dealt a difficult hand in life and made the best
with that hand instead of making excuses.
Reading is what helped me finish writing a book at 29-years-old.
Reading increases your vocabulary.
You may sometimes hear people using big words that you don't know,
and it's because they read, and you don't.
So, let's read more in order to learn more words
and become better communicators.

PLEASE LISTEN TO ME ON THIS!
I don't know you or your story or what you may be going through.
But I do know many of you are going through hell.
Sadly, some of you are victims of abuse and you don't understand
how this could happen to you. Many of you are going things
that your teachers, principals, or peers cannot even begin to relate too.
Some of your parents are in jail or prison and have missed a lot of your
childhood and many birthdays.
Some of y'all had childhoods cut short because your single parent put the
responsibility on you to step up to the plate.
Some of you young ladies and young boys are going to school every day,
and nobody knows that you have been abused by people in your own family.
Many of you cannot even celebrate Mother's Day or Father's Day
because your parents, for some reason or another, are not around anymore.
Some of your parents have even died in your arms.
You may feel alone and feel like there is no point in living.
I have at times experienced that level of pain, I have felt like harming myself
at times because I thought that was the easiest way to relieve all this misery.
Lil bro, lil sis, self-harm is not the easy way out.
If you seriously self-harm yourself, more people will be hurt.
Many of you have little brothers and little sisters that are counting on you.
I'm counting on you. I cannot tell you why what happened to you happened.
Some people get dealt good cards and some of us get dealt unfortunate
hands in life.
But no matter what hand you get dealt, if you strategize and want it bad
enough, you can make something out of the hand you were dealt.
Cry if you have to, but quitting and self-harming just because it's hard is not
an option. If you ride this out, you'll see that God has a plan for you.

- I HAVE A LOT OF TENACITY -

I remember a lady told me years ago that she loved
my tenacity.
At the time I didn't know what it meant until I went and
googled it.
Tenacity just means being determined.
In this life, you will need a lot of tenacity.
When you have that test that seems too hard
or when your plan just doesn't work out as expected,
you have to have tenacity to get
back up and do it again and again and again and again.
In other words, keep falling forward.
Tenacity is a must-have in this game of life.

- I AM UNBREAKABLE -

This whole book may seem like I'm saying the same thing.
I'm going over it like this because I want you to understand
that I understand that your life is real. Life can and
will throw some mean, hard, Mike Tyson level,
punches your way. If you are not strong mentally,
it will knock you out within the first two seconds.
Life doesn't always aim to hit you in the face.
It may hit you in the ribs, then it may uppercut you,
then come back up top and hit you in the head.
Life doesn't play fair and life does not care about you.
But if you study properly and mentally prepare for every
punch combination, dodge, and every trick that life
will try to throw at you to get you off course,
you will always be unstoppable and unbreakable.

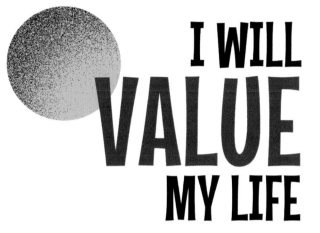

I WILL VALUE MY LIFE

You can go to the mall and buy another phone
to replace the one that you broke.
You can go buy yourself another pair of sneakers
and another pair after that pair.
You can have all the money in the world.
But even with all the money in the world,
you cannot buy one more second of your life.
Value your life because you only get ONE chance to live.
By all means, enjoy life and have fun,
but also know that you were created
to do something while here on this earth.
The world needs your gift.
You have a great purpose.
Figure it out and let's get to it.

- I WILL WIN -

I know life can be brutal,
but you are in control of your life.
Life doesn't have more power over you.
YOU CAN WIN in life.
I have failed over and over again in life.
I have burned bridges with some very important people.
I have made several poor business decisions.
But no matter what, I kept going and learning,
and eventually the light bulb went on
and I finally understood what I needed to do better.
I have always seen more for myself.
I always knew as early as 11 or 12
that there was more out there for me.
I got tired of losing and just taking what life
gave me every day.
It's at that moment that you get tired
of your situation when you make up your mind that,
come hell or high water,
I'm in this game to WIN IT ALL.

- I WILL BE XENIAL -

Xenial means being friendly or hospitable towards other people.
We tend to fear others based on differences
such as them being from another country, race, or culture.
We see other people in school or around us
who may look different, talk differently,
or may even eat different kinds of food.
Keep an open mind to other people
who are different from you.
You never know, that person who's different from you
may be the one you'll have to call on one day.

I know being grown seems like fun,
but I'm asking you to slow down.
Do not rush to be grown. Enjoy your youth.
You only get to be young once.
When you are young, you do not have to pay rent,
electricity bills, car insurance, gas bills, etc.
Your main job right now is just to go to school
and make decent grades.
Enjoy laughing with your homeboys and homegirls.
Enjoy cracking jokes with each other, enjoy riding bikes,
and going to the fair. Enjoy going to the mall,
getting that nice outfit and showing it off at the
movies or school.
Don't rush getting into serious relationships,
PLEASE TAKE YOUR TIME.
Once those youthful years are gone,
they are gone forever.

- I WILL STAY ZEALOUS -

To be zealous is to be passionate, committed,
and devoted to something.
We have talked about finding a good hobby,
finding a good legal hustle, learning what your gift is,
and being zealous about it.
Learn what that hobby, hustle, or gift is, study it, and
become the best to ever do it. If it's doing hair,
become the best stylist that ever lived.
If it's playing a sport, become better than any player
that ever played that sport.
Whatever you do, take pride in it. God gave you that gift
and He said that it will make room for you
and set you before great men.So, stay true to it.
This is my second book. I'm gifted to write,
and I'm gifted at talking to and inspiring people.
So, I encourage you to find you something
to be committed to and zealous about and get to it.

Made in the USA
Columbia, SC
22 May 2021